DEEP HUNGER

God Will Change Your Appetite Toward Him

Bill Vincent

RWG Publishing
PO Box 596
Litchfield, IL 62056
https://rwgpublishing.com/

Published in the United States of America

Paperback: 978-1-60796-958-7

Hardcover: 978-1-60796-964-8

I just really feel a spirit burden of intercession. This is something that came over me, the favor of God, and how God is breaking out and moving, specifically with revival and breakthrough in families like household salvation.

I believe in coming into agreement. So, we will agree as we release this right now. So, you need to declare that as for me and my house, we will serve the Lord. And Lord, I'm putting the responsibility on you to anoint the message and the messenger not to pass over, that I'm still contending and praying revival, the breakout in my home and my family. I'm asking for household salvation, God, we're going to proclaim liberty and an opening of the prison for those that are bound. Maybe you're praying for a son and a daughter, or a mother, or a brother, but go ahead with the corporate anointing that's here. Then say, God, we break every bondage and every chain of addiction, and whatever the blinding power of the god of this world is, we wanted to see that removed off the hearts and the veil torn right now. So, let the people say that our loved ones can come to know and have the revelation of Jesus right now.

We see the revelation of Jesus piercing the darkness; the light of the glorious truth of the gospel, piercing the darkness right now with the spirit of illumination and Revelation, opening the eyes and tearing back the veil where our hearts and minds are blinded because of the prince of this earth. And we command the door to be open, we proclaim liberty, and we call by your name, Jesus, and we claim the souls right now, God. We hold you to your word and your promise that if we decided to believe and follow you in love, you would be sure to send the message through the messenger to reach everybody in the rest of our family right now. So, we claim those souls in Jesus' name. Thank you, God, right now for those souls in Jesus' name. In this very moment, we say we declare and give birth to souls coming into the kingdom of God, and we remember today to pray for those that we love in our homes and our families. May they come to know Jesus Christ, that this would be the year of breakout salvation, that this would be the year of the Lord's favor, and that you would remember my brother and my sister and my aunt, my uncle and my cousin, and all the way down my blood by hand; that you would also remember today, God that we are praying. We're saying no to the works of darkness, no to fear, anxiety, and depression, no to the spirit of hopelessness and despair, and every other addiction, we are binding and locking and shutting the enemy down right now. And we are losing the kingdom of God and losing the great revelation of Jesus right now.

This is going to be the time where the power of God comes suddenly. And people have an interest, hunger, and an openness to the gospel that they never had before. That's what we need to contend for. That's what we need to pray for God that every person that I call my home and family would have an openness to the gospel and that the blinding power of the god of this world would no longer be able to blind them. We open up the door for them to come in freely; we open up the door for them to be able to see. And we call and release upon them the spirit of wisdom, revelation, and illumination in the knowledge of Christ as we think about this time, our families, it could be a hard, depressing time.

It's relational, and we've come into the revelation of the father, Abba Father, it's all about been in the kingdom of God's family. It's not just some organization or some church religion as we know it, but a family, and if you grew up in a broken home, and you don't have an image of a father; you don't have an image of how family works, then you feel others are very blessed to be closer with their family. It's time we remember those that we have to reach out to. I pray for the anointing of healing and reconciliation that you would begin to reconcile and restore, even a strange relationship. All this has to do with the type of hunger that this book is about.

So, I feel like there's a word from heaven right now. Here, the prodigal son and the daughter comes home, or somebody like the prodigal in your family calls after many years, maybe they suddenly wake up and say, listen, we're tired of living this way. We want to get back the intimacy, fellowship, and Communion, and you need to believe God for that because he breaks and removes the curse. I love how God breaks the curse that we see in Malachi 4, right after hundreds of years of darkness.

We go into what they call the darkness hundreds of years from the end of Malachi as we go into the light – I mean the glorious light of the gospel. And the Lord says, there's a curse on the land. And the reason is that the hearts of the fathers need to be restored to the daughters, and the hearts of the sons and daughters need to be restored to the fathers, and there's a brokenness in the land. And it has to do with the family. But, it's when you pray and use the atmosphere in the open heaven, and there's a specific moment of divine asking, there's also a particular moment of divine receiving. So, I'm using this moment of open Heaven, this moment of divine asking to get a divine receiving because the Bible says that in Mark 11 verse 24, whatever you ask for, when you pray, believe you will receive it.

So, I believe you are receiving what you've asked for right now. I'm receiving harvest and souls and revival in my family, I am receiving right now not one person, but I would call family by blood those who wouldn't have an opportunity to know Jesus. And yet, at the same time, you're not the one who is responsible always to reach them. You may have pushed them away, or push the way a son or a daughter in your zeal to see them know Jesus, you've got the reputation. And you're no longer an effective witness. You've got to trust that God said he would anoint the message in the messenger, and reach them with the gospel right now. God, there's not one person in my house, I want the Angel of Death to pass over right now because one lamb for one house, I've got the lamb because I've got the blood of the Lamb. As for me and my house, we will serve the Lord. Now, I declare and trust that you, God, will call the Angel of Death to pass over every other person that I called my bloodline and family. I claim their souls in Jesus' name. Amen.

Sometimes, you just got to tell the devil in the spiritual warfare part of it that we command those who are in captive to be set free, and the door to be open. And we proclaim liberty, and we rebuke the binding power of the god of this world. The Bible says that that spirit has blinded the hearts and the minds of every unbeliever. So, they can't see the penetrating, glorious light of the gospel. And that's what Christ came to announce that the great light has come. And that's the glorious gospel, and it's penetrating all the darkness. And so, God, we declare that a great light shall go forth from this place, and it'll be the glorious light of the gospel. And I want to be that burning shining lamp. I want to be that glorious burning lamp with the glorious light, and the witness and the love of Jesus in my heart and new way.

But, there is an anointing that goes out in the spirit, for those troubled on the water. Pray this and Say, God, I want to be a lighthouse, a city on a hill. God's restoring the salt right now. What happens when we lose our saltiness? God's restoring the salt, and he's restoring the light because you and I are the salt and the light of the earth. So, God, I pray right now for a fresh baptism of the Spirit of God that would bring our witness and make us salt and light as John, the Baptist, with a burning shining lamp. But may we have our love, zeal, and witness to reach people that need to know Jesus. And I just felt the Lord nudged me to say. It's like, there's an anointing here right now to pray for household salvation. To trust that God is going to break and remove the curse and restore the hearts of the father's and turn it to the children, and the hearts of the children to the fathers.

God, I thank you for the anointing that brings healing and reconciliation in homes and families. It's like a word of knowledge. Somebody needs to grab ahold of it because you're a strange son and daughter. Your prodigal son and daughter may know the Lord, but they're not talking to you. You need to believe that suddenly, it is going to happen from heaven after many years. And they're going to come home. The Lord was speaking to me about the prodigal son and daughter. It wasn't just the prodigal son and daughter sinner coming back to Christ, but also in homes and families where you need them to come home. Do you have that door open right now to receive back a reconciliation in some area of your life, family, or even divorce? Did you know God could bring healing back to the world? God brings restoration back to the world. So, we release that right now in Jesus' name. Amen.

There are many examples we have, even in the scriptures of these men and women that were ordinary like you and me, and we see what God did in and through them and the power of the Holy Spirit and the power of the gospel. And we realized we could do and preach the same message that we were born today for a reason for such a time as this. God didn't have you born, or designed your birth at any other time. He had you born today. It's about you. So, you might have wanted to live in the 1800s or the

1500s, or when the church was moving and birth 2000 years ago. Maybe you want to be living in the future, but you are living today. You were born for this time, and you were born for this purpose. It is great, and as much as we honor and remember what God did through all the great men and women revivalists and God generals and ministries of faith and power, we long and remember the glorious days. You are here, should the Lord tarry, or should the Lord returned in the next few generations, you would be the modern generation of the Apostle Paul's. You would be the modern generations of the Elisha, and the Elijah's the modern generations of the John G, Lake, and Smith Wigglesworth, and Kathryn Kuhlman. It would be you and me and our children's children.

So, it's okay to believe you're pretty important to God, and so is your destiny. God made you and me just a little lower than the angels. But, maybe we have something that they would even desire, Christ in you doesn't get better than Christ in me. I have Christ in me. God didn't save me to get me to Heaven Fire insurance. He saved me to get to heaven, and me manifesting and releasing it now. What should we do for all of eternity now? Very simple – Know him. Would you just put your hand on your heart and hunger for a moment and say, Lord, that's my desire. God, we want to know how to become steward atmospheres. We want to know how to host and make room for your presence. That's what we need. That's the transformation.

It's not the servants transforming people. It's not the programs. It's the presence and the power of God. Have you ever realized you needed a fresh baptism of the Holy Spirit fire? I've needed a fresh anointing to touch me again so that I could touch the masses. Lord, let me drip with the honey, the oil, and the wine. I want to be able to go into places and cities and regions and bring transformational glory. We never rush and hurry the presence of God, rush on to the next part of the program or service. You would get all that you need if you could have an encounter with the presence of God and hunger for him – spiritual hunger, real-raw hunger. Even when we're tired, even when we're weary, we can say. Lord, quicken me to call on your name. The Holy Spirit will do it. Come and manifest and reveal Jesus to me; the Holy Spirit will do it. No man can say that Jesus is Lord but by the Spirit of God. You must depend upon the Holy Spirit so that you can even draw near unto him. But if you draw near unto me, I will draw near unto you.

One of the first promises I remember when I got saved is if I drew near unto God, God would draw near unto me. If you seek me and search for me with all of your heart, and that was the question for me. Am I seeking and searching with all of my heart? You will find me. Jesus said, if you Love me and you love my command, we will come and make our home and our habitation with you. He said to me, and the father will manifest ourselves to you. That's John 15. If you love me, and you love my word, and you abide in me, and my words abide to do, we will manifest ourselves to you. That's not just a future manifestation. How many are praying that Jesus would manifest himself? We're theological. We're intelligent, but we want so much more. We want Jesus to reveal himself unto us.

How can you show yourself to me? Moses prayed, please show me your glory. It seemed he saw the power of God, but he still said, Show me your glory. You got the pillar of cloud by day and the pillar of fire by night. You got the angel of the Lord before you try to go to your enemies, manna from heaven, quail from heaven, and every other sign and wonder. And yet Moses said, show me your glory. That's my prayer. Show me your glory. God, I want to see the inner reality of who you are. Have you ever desired that kind of closeness and intimacy with somebody, it could be a husband or a wife? How much more is there to know that I could spend a lifetime with you, and I'd still want to know more? And to think that for all of eternity, the vastness, right? The unsearchable riches of Christ.

So, we exalt you tonight, Jesus, come on, can we do that? Just one more moment of just bumping in and exalting him and thanking Him and desiring for more.

Maybe when I pray for people that want prayer, we could pray for healing. But why don't we pray for the gift of the Holy Spirit? That you would become the flame that would be the Blaze. I've been in a constant need for revival and renewal and refreshing. I could only imagine how much the church needs it if the preacher needs it more. I think it's when we feel we don't need more. We're okay, and we're on fire. That was one of the greatest sins when the church didn't say that they needed everything. That they thought they were hot, and they were lukewarm cold. They lost the lamp of their first love. Had to say resort to be the lamp, the burning, and they thought they were burning. It said I counsel you to buy gold from me; we find in the fire turned in your filthy rags in your righteousness and coming to receive the fire. The gold in the fire, you remember that? And then, he said to him who overcomes if you have all these great promises? One promise was that you would eat of the fruit of the tree of life in God's paradise, freely.

Go back to the garden, the way it was garden and have access restored to the tree. And you can eat freely as much as you want to. That means you get to encounter and experience the knowledge; the wisdom cases as much as you wish, you may freely eat of the tree of the fruit. Is it possible to walk with God to such a degree like Adam in the beginning, that you are no longer conscious of the fact that you're naked, that you're hiding? You're no longer conscious of the fact that this is right or wrong or sin, you're just so restored. That all you can think about is the available glory, the intimacy. That is why Christ redeemed me, not just fire insurance, get me out of hell to heaven, but to get me back to my original purpose, to walk and to know him. Also, to walk and talk in the cool breeze of the garden without any separation. What separates you and me today is church, religion, and interpretation and the business of life and brokenness and sin, but if we knew how far the hunger, friendship, and intimacy with God would take you, then a modern generation of you know people that know God's like Enoch, to walk with God like Enoch and Like Adam. I want to walk with God; I want to be a friend of God, shall I hide from Abraham and my friend what I'm doing?

The Lord has been speaking to me about the need for the church to fall in love with Jesus again. In Matthew 7, We think it's a rebuke for the false prophets, and the false teachers do miracles in my name and cast out demons in my name, all these are great signs and wonders of my name. And the Lord said on that day, depart from me for I do not know you. And I said, who is it that you do not know Lord, the sinner, the unbeliever, the False Prophet? And he said, No, these are believers. These are Christians that learn to cast out demons and move in the supernatural, in the prophetic and do all these great kingdom exploits. They must have known me, but it says they don't know me.

So, I did a study on the word "depart from me," for I never knew that "you" in the word means you cease to be known. It's like the end of a marriage or relationship. Have you ever had a friendship, and you thought you'd be best friends forever? You ever have seen the tragedy of divorce or the end of a relationship after 20 years? How about all that anger, and now, it's the ex-wife or the ex-husband, and you never thought there'd be a day you weren't in love. You never thought there'd be a day that that relationship would end this way. You lost something, that's what Jesus is saying that what we had now become that lukewarm or cold, not hot. And you need to say restore to me the land for my first love because you've lost that first love. Those are the ones that he's saying, depart from me. Could it be that many of us will get to heaven on that day, even some of our favorite preachers we see on TV or those that did the most works? And you hear the Lord say; I never knew you because you cease to be known, you let go with the intimacy and the closeness and the love we had. You continue to do all the work. So, the kingdom you were a faithful member of the church in Revelation, he first said, here's where you've been faithful. And then he says, here's what you need to repent. And here's the reward if you overcome.

Do you know that overcoming is a process, and through the spirit of overcoming, you are an overcomer? Though a righteous man falls and stumbles seven times, he rises again. Are you an overcomer? Are you fighting? Do you have something you're battling with? There was always what the church did right. But in the end, it was what the church needed to repent of.

My greatest fear as a Christian isn't sin or unrepentant sin. I trusted the grace of God, and in the finished work of God. I trust in the blood; my greatest sin is, depart from me. I never knew you because you cease to be known because you no longer make yourself available in communion and fellowship and intimacy. You got a dead works prayer life. And there are people in church today, and the only reason we connect in church is to get our blessing, get our healing, get our prophetic word, get out by 9. You could probably say repent, restore me to the lap of my first love because we seriously need revival and awakening in our hearts if you don't hear the spirit of what I'm preaching. We are all in danger of the most simple truth the Lord gave us, didn't he? Love the Lord your God with all your heart, mind, soul, and strength. And what does loving the Lord your God look like? Love your neighbor as you love yourself.

Now, you have an appetite for things you didn't like before, incredible. And I don't mean to offend anybody. But how many remember reading the Book of Proverbs, you know the wife of your youth, the first love, the bride's, and the bridegroom. And here's the bridal covenant with Jesus where the bridegroom is the bride, and then the Lord gives us so many parables and allegories about the church and the love and the great mystery and how you love your wife, or your bride is how you love Christ and Christ loved the church. How about this one, he said that the wife of your youth, let her satisfy you with her breasts continually. You know, God's called the many breasted one, Almighty God.

The moment the Lord no longer is your source, the fountain of living waters, you will have an appetite to be satisfied with everything else. When your desire is him and him alone, God's not trying to get you to get holy to get away from all your pleasures. He's trying to get you to love him wholeheartedly. So, you can know the pleasure that's in the fullness of them. Every other pleasure is under the pleasure of loving and knowing him. The Lord was speaking to me about the need for the church to return to the secret place of his presence and begin to have real intimacy again. That's even some of the greatest problems of men and women of God, you know.

They might have known more about God, more about the church, more about how to run church and ministry, and more about the business of ministry and more about the work of revival. But in the end, they knew God less than they did in the beginning because they were known; it's like the loveless marriage. And how does it even get there one day when you wake up, and you realize, Thank You, Jesus. He is a covenant-keeping God, and He never gives up on you and me. But the whole message of the wise Virgin and the foolish virgin. The wise virgins knew how to take an extra supply of oil with them. They knew there would be a day with the oil, and the lamps would not be burning. And there were those burning that their oil was out. They said, give us some of yours. And they said no, you've got to go to the bridegroom when you can. And why is it that you didn't just fill your lamp? Why is it you didn't get overflow and take an extra supply of oil with you, we need to learn in this day how to take an extra supply. We need not be dependent upon somebody else's gift anointing and mantle. We need to be the reason there is oil.

We need to know how to go to the bridegroom. We need to know how to go to the master. Do you hunger, have a need, or want to encounter and experience the presence of God because you can? You can have as much of Jesus now as you want to, what a fantastic thought! That it's just sometimes us and our lack of hunger or we're convinced in some other beguiled tradition or religion that we can't have more. And we got some messed up idea of what encountering God's look like, because of whatever pain or wound, and there is grace for these things. But we have to learn that we can have the Father, who gives the Holy Spirit freely to those who ask him, he's not holding back. I want to know you, Jesus.

And the great Apostle Paul, that I might know him and the power of his resurrection, I want to know him. And I want to know the power of his resurrection about just his future resurrection with the power of his resurrection now and the fellowship of his sufferings, so that I can be conformed to the image. I have one desire to be like Christ. Do you imagine that you can be transformed into the very image of Christ? That's why Jesus said, if you've seen me, you've seen the Father. What if he said, can you see the father and me? I'm a work in progress. I think I've tried doing church and religion, ministry too hard and too long. And then, in the end, you go, I don't even know you. I'm burned out on the very thing that I love and serve because I no longer have those mornings, or days or weeks of extended times, where it's just the presence of God, like I got to a place in the business of my life and ministry, where I've preached 300 times a year. So, I need to get prophetic stuff, words of knowledge, get prepared for services, and get ready. Somewhere along the lines, it was no longer about God. It was about what I had to get. I was always in a place of getting ready. And I never could tell if I loved the Lord in my agenda and motive. I wanted to be the anointed speaker, the most prophetic with the best word of knowledge. See, everybody touched and healed. It wasn't until I got so broken and lost everything.

I fell in love with Jesus again. And I realized if I never went back into what we call, you know, ministry and preaching, I was going to love the Lord, and not love the Lord when I need a job or love the Lord when they need to get healed. We do have these things that drive us, don't wait. But what did Job say in his brokenness and pain and great trial, though you have slain me, I will trust you. The beauty and brokenness, right? The Lord does draw near to those of a broken and a contrite heart. I think that's what fasten works when you do it right because you're not just humbling yourself, there is an amount of pain and weakness.

You know what, in everything that I've said, do you know how easy it is to say, I love you, Jesus, turn back? Beat my brow and go back to the beginning of the line, make penance for all the years. We tend to make penance. Even the whole idea of repentance came from the word penance.

And though we know that that's gone and forgotten, and for people to grow, we steal one another to each other in practice, do penance. But how do we know you're repentant? Church leaders will say something, you know, in a day where all these accusations are coming out, scandals are coming out. And I believe women can come forward; I believe men can come forward, I believe injustice can come forward. But what about when the line is crossed, and a man said, I'm not guilty and wrote a suicide letter, a man of influence and politics with several accusations. And even if he was repentant and changed, he's found guilty and committed suicide, and he left a note for his family.

Whether you consciously do it or not, we have this barter system with God. I call it a transaction. Do you know the Old Testament, New Covenant?

People try to bring the old to the new, and well, the old is done. And I'm just kind of the new and grace, how do you bring together the old and the new? How many of you know what the old was? It's a transaction; you do this, and I'll do that. God gave a promise. He said, if you do this, I will do that transaction, far bargain.

The new covenant changed in this one thing, the biggest thing, Jesus, but in this one thing, relationship. The new covenant is relational. It's now the father relating to sons, based on the fact that you are a son, and not based on… I'll do this if you do this. It's now all in Christ. It's now on I am a son, I'm a daughter and a joint-heir. I have a father, Abba, Father; it's a relationship. That's why there is, therefore, now no sentence, no guilt, no condemnation, no shame. But yet, we measure ourselves even one to another, or how we respond to the presence of God. How we engage your pressing to the presence of God, based on how worthy we feel that day or week, or moment, just because we don't know, or we do. But we just not by experience of revelation know that you can have as much of Jesus now as you want to, and that we're not made to have this, measuring where we keep track of moments and hours and how many chapters and how many weeks of devotion and how faithful we are. There's none righteous, not one.

Have you ever asked yourself? Sin is sin, but why? There were some things I know I had to repent from. And I thought Lord that said, but you just called it said, why is that sin? I repent because it is a sin. I'm going to; you're better than me. We know the wages of sin is death. But if none are righteous, no not one, and all the fallen short, then sin is a sin. Drunkenness, adultery, party, you committed murder, anger in your heart, you put it on the same level, you made lust in the heart of the same level of adultery. We're all adulterers. God did away with the system of how we go; you're a murderer. You're an adulterer. And he said, well if you have anger in your heart with your brother or offense or bitterness, you're now a murderer. So, therefore, you're as guilty as the murderers.

The Lord did say that because he was saying sin is sin, so, the ever processed out loud and asked why is this sin? Gossip is a sin. We know the pain and consequence of sins, but why God said it's a sin is that this wasn't we as we live our whole life navigating, confessing, and repenting of our sin? And then, why is it that we have appetite? Why is it that we wander and are told you have forsaken the fountain of living waters? Does it go if you want to be free from guilt, condemnation, and shame and focus on to love me? Peter, do you love me? Yes, Lord, I love you. You know that I don't ask if you love me by association and closeness and proximity. I want to ask you, Peter, do you love me in this second time? Yes, Lord, I love you.

Yeah, I'm not even talking about like, bro love and friendship love. I'm saying Peter, do you love me, and the Lord? You know, Peter looked at the Lord a third time, really puzzled. What do you mean? Do I love you? Because he just kept hearing the same thing. His understanding of love, his revelation of the Lord was talking about the covenant family never give up love. I'm not looking for well, that's a friend. Well, is that a close friend or an associate? Is that a best friend? Or is that family love will you know, there are different ways that we love. I love my wife; I love my daughters. I love my team. I love Christians. We say I love you. But I don't love you like I love my wife.

So, Peter was confused, as the Lord brought the revelation of love to him, and it does come down to loving the Lord your God with all your heart, mind, soul, and strength. And my greatest fear was God, am I repenting enough? Am I confessing enough and day to day, week to week? Do I remember the sins of omission in the sense of commission? And the Lord said you wouldn't even need to worry if you love me. David was an adulterer and a murderer, and you don't excuse the sin. But how about this one, the Lord said, but he loved me, and his heart was after my heart. I'm going to make that guy King. And what would we do with the murder of an adulterer in the church today? Like Paul, the apostle, Chief sinner, murderer. And the church had ideas about when Paul tried to come back.

We're gonna have to love a lot of ugly people that are going to come back. And you're going to go, man, your sexual abuser, beat your wife. You gotta come back; you're a liar. You're drunk; you're an alcoholic man, we put labels and types on. You can never overcome those things. Sometimes. We see it play out in the media now. Then years later, 20 years later, these are things you didn't say to me. It's like when does it stop?

How is it that the media is the judge and jury? And yet, is God exposing things? Absolutely, but somewhere in the midst of it all, we should probably draw a line and go. Okay, guys, great. If there's anybody else that needs to come out, they should all come out now. So, we could move on and no person that's ever been hurt or wounded or a victim or abused or taken advantage of sexually should have to live without that pain and not be able to come forward, I get that. But it's become some are now circus. Not everybody else's sins are on the media. It brings you back to this question. When a man is caught in a trespass, you are spiritual, restore. How does that work in the Bible? Matthew 18, if you find one, you go to your brother in private. If he doesn't receive, you go to your church leaders. If they don't receive you, then go to the church.

We expose, and in the end, we don't redeem and recover. So, that's where I've been on my journey, and my greatest fear is, in the end, I'll have done all this great work and preach the ministry and hear "depart from me, I never know you." When I know the Lord and again more or did, I was very good at the gifts he gave me. And in the end? Did you learn to love, restore to me the lamp of my first love? I won't have to worry about all the other sins and repenting and confessing, and embedding and confessing because I won't have an appetite. If I'm in love with Jesus, shouldn't you be so consumed with being consumed by the one? Not getting yourself ready, the bride makes herself ready. But the Bible says the king gave everything she needed to get ready. Remember, when Esther made herself ready? Six months in the oil, six months in the perfume, the King made provision for everything she needed and all the other virgins to make themselves ready. How many of you know the King, Jesus has made everything we need to get ready for his purpose available. And not only did the king give everything they needed, but it also says he gave an allowance, that was grace to receive and apply the grace of the provision to partner together with what God has finished.

Look at this when we say, I'm not praying. I haven't read my Bible in six months, and I hate to go to church right now. So, how do you want to love God in that way? Well, you know what, Lord, I want to go back to the world. I want to go back to Egypt like the rest of them did in Israel; they all wanted to go back. And we think about how you could want to go back after he brought you out? How many times did Israel want to go back under Moses? I said you want to go back to what you have ever just had as a struggle. You know, the temptation is never a sin, it's when you get that revelation because you're tempted doesn't mean you sin. I said, God, I'm tempted right now. I'm so mad at the church, you know, years ago, I said I'm so mad at the church. I want to go out and drink every day. How about that? Because I want to love you right there.

I haven't even been to the church of God in six months. I want to love you there. I'm not praying; I'm not holy. I'm not. I want to love you there. God, I'm in the divorce, I want to love you there. Can God love people there? Without the idea that you have to accept sin. No. I struggle with this homosexuality as an act, not as people. Somebody says I'm a lesbian, or I'm gay, I go well, you know, I get a little homophobic. That's just my upbringing. God or not, God, it's not because I'm a preacher, and it's not religion. I get weird about men and men and women and women.

God wants to reach you where you are.

And then, having to love the person and stand by the truth of my standard. We think we got to bring down the standard to hold on to our truth and grace. I have love grace for people. I'm like, come on in; you're smoking outside, go ahead and smoke until you are free. I don't want to come to your church; I don't have anything good to wear. Good, don't worry, just come like that.

So many Christians in the church today. The church is full of religious Christians that do so right and heresy a hundred type-checking your theology every day and every week, and in the end, they have no love and no passion and no Grace. Just true. Did you learn to love? And do you learn to love the Lord your God? So, let me just read, and I'm going to finish with this: Psalm 63, the heart of David. Spirit, the mighty warrior that worship our God, had to go to the caves. The only men that came to him were 400 men broke, discontent, outcasts; nobody else wanted with the only man that saw what was on David came, in the desert, in the wilderness, in the caves, didn't look like King, didn't feel like King. And yet, it was David that said, touch not the Lord's anointed, Saul. And all that David did to love the man that just wanted to have him killed, chased him was chasing him. David is in this place. You know it wasn't too long ago. Samuel had the whole horn of oil anointed him among all his brothers. And he remembered the anointing, he remembered the word, and I'm sure there were days David felt the disappointment, the discouragement, when and how and he looked out over the dirt. The ragtag group doesn't look like a king of a palace. And he's in this place that you might call the valley or the wilderness, the night of the soul, and David makes a great declaration. He says God; you are my God early will I seek you diligently, consistently. Every morning early, I will seek you. And I thought that when I seek God, sometimes, every day not just to get ready to preach. Though you have slain me, I will trust you, God, you are God. I will seek you. Not because I'm looking for a kingdom or a palace, the unfulfilled vision and dream, but just God, you are my God. And I am committed every day to the passionate pursuit of seeking you early.

My soul thirsts for you. My flesh longs for you. You know it's okay to desire God in your flesh. Your soul, your heart, your mind, my flesh even longs in the dry and thirsty land where there is no water. Water being the Holy Spirit. I'm in a dry and thirsty place or season, and there is no water, and here's what David wanted. It's what I want. I have looked for you in the sanctuary to see your power and glory. Sometimes, all you want is to see his power. You want to see his glory, but you're in a dry and thirsty land where there is no water. This is when you say, God, you are my God, early will I seek you in a dry and thirsty land where there is no water. When I want to see your power and glory, I will seek you though you have slain me. I will trust you, knowing that I have all the unanswered questions about my disappointment and discouragement and why I'm not healed and why you didn't break through, why you didn't answer faith and mystery. God, you are my God, I will seek you because your loving kindness is better than life, my lips will praise you. You saved me. You're never to do anything.

Loving-kindness is better than life. And then, he says, I will bless you while I live. I will lift my hands and my soul in your name. As soon as she makes a declaration in verse 5, my soul will be satisfied with marrow and fatness, and my mouth will praise you with joyfulness. David knew the key to having his soul satisfied with fatness and marrow was when you could say God, you are my God, I will love you, and I will seek you even amid my enemies, night of the soul, even in dry and thirsty land. I will love you; I will praise You, I will lift my hands in your name because you're worthy even when I don't understand what I'm facing even though I don't understand where I am, and why I'm in the caves. I'm going to trust it's easy to pray some significant breakthrough in revival and healing, but to praise him in the wilderness. I've ever had to seek God like this, draw near like the heavens were brass, and trying to get God to come down or try to get up to, at least, where God was. Have you ever felt silence distance? Is he enough to say God you are my God early? Passionate pursuit and pressing in. I'm hungry.

David said, my soul. I don't know when, but it's coming. In the valley, when you can lift your hands in his name, in the pain when you can lift your hands. It's coming to my soul, salvation satisfied with fatness and marrow. I know the key to turning my wilderness into rivers, in the desert, turning my desert into pools in the desert is when I can praise Him. Even when I'm in a dry and thirsty land where there is no waterman, it's hard to pray and get breakthrough and go after the things of God when you're this broke and struggling and sick, and you're not sensing the nearness of God.

And then look at what David said. I think this is the key here to verse 6: when I remember you on my bed, and I meditate on you in the night watches, sometimes, I just got to stop. I remember the feeding of the 5000, remember the feeding of the 4000, remember the breakthrough, remember the healing, remember the faithfulness, remember the works when he brought me out of the land of Egypt, remember the manna, remember the Quail, remember when Israel did not remember, saying they forgot his works. They turned back in the day of battle. Because they forgot his works, they did not remember his power. That David said, here's the key in the midst of what I'm facing today. I must remember every other time that God spoke and every other time that God healed and every other time that God rescued and say that is the faithfulness of loving kindnesses. There is something that I do when I get a little disappointed or discouraged or down and get depressed and tired and lazy and don't want to go after it.

There's an atmosphere that changes and breaks out, everything else follows. How many of you could say with me tonight? God, you are my God, I'm gonna seek you again, the way that I used to. That hunger with that passion. Let me love you in the end, as I loved you in the beginning. I want the fire back?

So, you know it's not a denial that you're in a place of disappointment, anger, or discouragement, you are in the caves, you are in the wilderness, you're in the desert, and Saul's trying to kill you. You did have an anointing. Samuel anointed you and did have a prophetic word you did have. You know what could have been 40 days, and we make it 40 years, why? How we respond. Sometimes, you got to put the board back on the throne, and you got to dethrone things that happened in our lives that we have no power over. The only thing we have power over now is choice. But, what we're going to do with what we have as far as moving forward.

Sometimes, we can't get off the throne, what happened when we were younger, or we let things have authority over us all the time, or chip over us all the time because we are the ones that have a choice. You ever met somebody that's just grieving, and it's normal, then you meet somebody that is grieving, and they're well beyond the time that we should be grieving and mourning, and they can't get free. The victim that cannot get free; we tend to blame, or we tend to look at everything as if it's outside of our control, and really, it's on our throne. We're empowering it. We've got to dethrone and make choices we can choose today to be free from decisions that we've made because of what happened when we were younger in the Lord, without believing in the inner healing. But, I believe some people are in constant need of getting healed, given too much power to the thing that hurt them. And they could never get out from under them. And others have never met somebody strong, or a survivor they've survived way more than we've had two people that came out of the Holocaust and out of war, they come back from war, and you think of what they had to live through every day. And then, we get this perspective, and we go, man. I just kind of worried about this, you know, problem at school, and then you get a real dose sometimes from people that were like captured by ISIS and tortured; sex slave and they get out your perspective, and then they seem to be so strong, and we can barely get over what happened in the seventh grade. I think a whole lot of churches have gotten this honestly, which is what has lordship in your life that you've kept on the throne that the lord should have had.

It's not a denial of the need for healing or inner healing, but I think if we could just partner sometimes with the strength that's in him, we would be able to move on, and let go that pain and that division and that unforgiveness and that offense and make that choice. So, I want to choose something today, God, you are my God, and early will I seek you. Can you do that today? I am not a victim of the circumstance and situation, and though you have slain me, I will trust you.

I think if you can lift your hands in his name in the situation, and you could say my soul will be satisfied. I know it will be, I know in your wilderness, in your desert, in your night of the soul, if you could say, I'm going to lift my hands in your name anyways and praise you anyway. So, even in the dry and thirsty land where there is no water, I'm going to live as if I've had a breakthrough when I need a break, I need a breakthrough, I need a healing break. I need a financial breakthrough, but you can feel the agenda and the pressure sometimes where people can't get or wait to receive whatever their expectation is. And it could never get up so high that it goes beyond me, myself, and I too, giving him the worthy praise that he deserves. In the midst of it all, even when you're in the caves and your enemies trying to kill you.

If you listen to the way we talk something and we just you know Oh man, this is happening right the warfare is against me what they're saying to my family, and you know, it's hard all through that. But don't put him on the throne. Don't give it so much lordship. Don't let your whole life, you know; there are people that I have that I know I call them builders. You got managers, and then you got good people that are just good at their work for you for 25, 35 years. And that's it, praise God, we need those two, but what is it about those that breakthrough and pioneer and start a business and you just like work for the man? Why is it that there's just those that find it easier to not battle and fight. You're always going to have those that manage; you're always going to have those that kind of work and serve. But there's a spirit I believe for the overcomer.

This is the difference sometimes between fighters and survival people, leaders, and then the ones that follow. I believe that the leadership is in Christ, I believe Christ as a head that people can rise into their full potential and the spirit of the overcomer. I love the fight, the good fight of faith, so people have to fight.

Do you know what happens with you? You don't ever experience a trial or a habit of breaking like a fall, healing, restoration. There's always with that scandal a shame, a heaviness; it's kind of over the building over the atmosphere just kind of the years can go by. But then you get that label in the spirit.

I feel like the Lord gave me a promise and set up Isaiah 61 verse 7, that instead of your shame and fear and confusion, you would have double, double honor, a double portion, double inheritance in this place.

And you too can have double portion honor, double portion inherited, a double portion of joy and not have to identify with the pain in the name of your sin or your divorce or your bankruptcy or your struggle or whatever it was you had to overcome as a

Christian. Whether people know about it publicly or not, you don't have to wear that Samson's Shame. His hair grew back, and he had double honor; in the end, they took out twice as many enemies. We should pray for the spirit of Samson – Spirit-might in the church.

You know, Jesus called people full of grace and truth, not one or the other. He was truth and grace at the same time. He could be a friend of sinners and uphold the truth. So, don't let your truth go. Don't let your standard of what you call holiness, righteousness, don't let it go. It's true, but Jesus was full of grace and truth. You can't be either one or the other. Love truth, a half-truth. Truth matters. So, it is grace. When you try to love people, or you do not love them as you try when you're trying to reach people in your truth without grace, they're like Mom, don't judge me that's why you don't have a voice at Christmas dinners anymore because you're always the religious guy, that's going to come in and tell them everything wrong, why they're all going to hell and now you have no voice. I'm going to preach anyways. Lord, I want to be somebody full of grace and truth, truth, and grace. God, you are my God early. Well, I think I know I'm speaking to somebody. I speak to myself and maybe feel a need for just revival in your prayer life and intimacy and love for God, and I'm trying to get my life's message. I want to pray for those that want the gift of the presence and hunger, and the grace to seek God. It is time to get hungry for more of God!

***

About the Author

Bill Vincent is no stranger to understanding the power of God. Not only has he spent over twenty years as a Minister with a strong prophetic anointing, but he is now also an Apostle and Author with Revival Waves of Glory Ministries in Litchfield, IL. Along with his wife, Tabitha, he leads a team providing apostolic oversight in all aspects of ministry, including service, personal ministry, and Godly character.

Bill offers a wide range of writings and teachings from deliverance to experiencing the presence of God and developing Apostolic cutting edge Church structure. Drawing on the power of the Holy Spirit through years of experience in Revival, Spiritual Sensitivity, and deliverance ministry, Bill now focuses mainly on pursuing the Presence of God and breaking the power of the devil off of people's lives.

His books 50 and counting has since helped many people to overcome the spirits and curses of Satan. For more information or to keep up with Bill's latest releases, please visit www.revivalwavesofgloryministries.com. To contact Bill, feel free to follow him on twitter @revivalwaves.

Recommended Books

By Bill Vincent

Overcoming Obstacles

Glory: Pursuing God's Presence

Defeating the Demonic Realm

Increasing Your Prophetic Gift

Increase Your Anointing

Keys to Receiving Your Miracle

The Supernatural Realm

Waves of Revival

Increase of Revelation and Restoration

The Resurrection Power of God

Discerning Your Call of God

Apostolic Breakthrough

Glory: Increasing God's Presence

Love is Waiting – Don't Let Love Pass You By

The Healing Power of God

Glory: Expanding God's Presence

Receiving Personal Prophecy

Signs and Wonders

Signs and Wonders Revelations

Children Stories

The Rapture

The Secret Place of God's Power

Building a Prototype Church

The breakthrough of Spiritual Strongholds

Glory: Revival Presence of God

Overcoming the Power of Lust

Glory: Kingdom Presence of God

Transitioning to the Prototype Church

The Stronghold of Jezebel

Healing After Divorce

A Closer Relationship With God

Cover Up and Save Yourself

Desperate for God's Presence

The War for Spiritual Battles

Spiritual Leadership

Global Warning

Millions of Churches

Destroying the Jezebel Spirit

Awakening of Miracles

Deception and Consequences Revealed

Are You a Follower of Christ

Don't Let the Enemy Steal from You!

A Godly Shaking

The Unsearchable Riches of Christ

Heaven's Court System

Satan's Open Doors

Armed for Battle

The Wrestler

Spiritual Warfare: Complete Collection

Growing In the Prophetic

Faith

The Angry Fighter's Story

Understanding Heaven's Court System

Restoration of the Soul

Spiritual Warfare Made Simple

Aligning With God's Promises

Web Site:

www.revivalwavesofgloryministries.com